SILENT TEARS

Compiled by
SHAMIS D-ASHUR

Illustrations by
ZARRIN AL-MOSTAFA

ISBN 0 9514858 0 6

Contents

INTRODUCTION

This booklet has arisen out of the need to support further the case for the eradication of female genital mutilation internationally and in Britain.

It has been conceived with a certain methodology in mind , i.e. to let the first hand experiences of women affected by infibulation and other types of mutilations to filter through the text in a series of interviews and statements. These interviews were compiled by workers of the London Black Women Health Action Project (to which we will refer from now on by its initials, the LBWHAP) with the consent of the women involved, maintaining however anonimity whenever required. These women are from several East African countries, living now in London, in particular in Tower Hamlet where the project operates from.

We want this to be at the forefront of this work, both in terms of the need to readdress the euro-centric and racist views in current European material on female genital mutilation, as well as, and most importantly in order to give an opportunity to black women affected by these practices to 'speak' for themselves about their experiences, to make the latter available to everybody to read in order to expand the work for eradication and the general understanding of the issues involved. For that reason only there seem to be an apparent lack of structure, however in order to help with the reading and understanding of the issues involved I have arranged all interviews and statements by themes. This was done primarily by the LBWHAP and Shamis Dirir Ashur in particular, I would also like to point out that any adjustment made afterwards has always undergone a consultative process.

I would like to underline that this is not specifically an international study on female genital mutilation or an academic study of the latter but it is about the subject along more generalised lines for contextual reasons, about the experience of African women living in Britain as mentioned earlier and the work undertaken by the LBWHAP, although links at international level will appear necessary in some sections of this book as work for the eradication of female circumcision is undertaken in many parts of the world in various degrees, it is also an important and positive factor in the expansion and reiteration of the programme for eradication.

This work will also comprise explanations and personal insights into the health complications of female genital mutilation and although not medically oriented, it is important to grasp (as we will see from some of the personal experiences) the extensive and long term damaging effects. We will see that the health complications manifest themselves in two stages: the immediate and the long term one.

In this introduction I would also like to affirm what has always been the position of the LBWHAP and which has been stated in all the printed material produced by the project, from annual reports to newsletters, to educational pamphlets: i.e that female circumcision can only be understood if it is firmly placed in the overall context of black women's health and the specific problems they face, from the NHS to health professionals in general who deal with them, as well as language difficulties and unawareness of certain rights within the NHS.

In short we must not forget the wider problems of racism, and how the physical and mental health services often choose to ignore the effects of racism and isolation on black women.

I would like to close this introduction by repeating in some ways what I have just mentioned above. The factor which contributes to make the debate and resolution of female circumcision more difficult, both in this country and the countries where it is still practiced on a large scale, is coming to terms with the painful issue which relates to the feeling of alienation and rejection from one's own culture, for example if one rejects circumcision, as well as the loss of status and consequently economic power for the women concerned as stated by their societies (and ours on the whole - possibility of marriage, integration, cultural identity, etc). Or as in some cases, the painful acceptance of domination through mutilation as well as health problems if accepted as part of one's cultural and religious make-up.

The problems linked with either decision are more acute given the special circumstances of an immigrant community as it is the case in London and elsewhere in Britain, where the support network and cultural identification is clearly played out all the time against the dominant British culture.

In the words of one woman interviewed:

"If we denounce it and say we want to stop, our families are outraged. It changes our position in our families. We can't win. If we circumcise our daughters there is pain. If we don't circumcise our daughters there is different pain. The community will not accept us. Discussions need to include how to stop. The main thing is to get people to see the problem, to see that it is a problem."

1. THE 'BARE' FACTS

It is important to mention if only briefly the 'bare' facts about female genital mutilation and the types undertaken by different communities and countries:

1) Circumcision proper entails the cutting of the prepuce or hood of the clitoris, it is also known by Muslem people as the 'Sunna'. This could properly be called female circumcision (although we will be referring and interchanging meaning to the other two types as well and use the term more generally used for the entire practice, i.e. female circumcision) unlike the other two types outlined below.

2) Excision/clitoridectomy is the partial or total removal of the clitoris and all or part of the labia minora (small lip) as well as the adjacent tissues of the labia majora (big lip), without the closing of the vulva.

3) Infibulation (Pharaonic circumcision), the most serious of mutilations: it means the total removal of the clitoris, of the labia majora and minora, (both lips) and the joining of the two sides of the vulva by stitching together. The amount of tissue removed and the extent of sewing varies from culture to culture. With the vulva sewn a small opening is left for menstrual flow and the passing of urine.

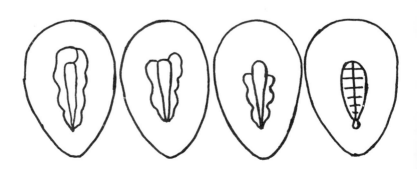

2. ORIGINS AS CONTROL OF FEMALE SEXUALITY

It has so far been impossible to establish the exact origins of female circumcision, however one thing has been clear: its purpose, i.e. the suppression and concealment of female's sexual life. It is not our purpose here to trace all the links which make up the origins however enlightening and worthwhile a task, a task which we may intraprend at a latter stage of our existence as a group.

However, we feel it is important to make a relativistic case for female circumcision and the societies which practice it in contemporary times (mainly African countries), not to condone its practice but to remember that other forms of controlling women's sexual lives had been and are in use in different cultures worldwide.

These forms are too numerous to mention but an example which forcefully reminds us of the similarity of such way of controlling women was the genital surgery (clitoridectomy) performed in certain western countries to cure what were considered women's problems: masturbation, nymphomania, hysteria, etc.

I mentioned this in order to remind us how too often what seems less serious forms of oppression (because determined by the so called civilizing powers) are in fact part of the same debilitating process and pressures that women suffer from the patriarchal society.

The confusion on the origins and the cultural and economic pressures which allow the practice to continue are some of the things uttered in the following extracts of interviews and statements (some of which are uttered in third person), - all the chapters will contain what in the introduction we termed first hand experiences - this process is happening so much that an identification process takes place and practices like female circumcision have become part of 'women's culture' in certain societies.

1. "I really don't know where it comes from, but I think from the Egyptians. It's Somali women's culture, it's part of one's life".

2. Nawal says that it was the turning point in her life. "The circumcision either makes you really angry or one becomes so passive that one continues in the role mapped out. It is another form of construction. Women are constructed for reproduction and man's pleasure. Her whole life is planned. From birth to death - it's settled".

3. "If they don't do it men won't get a virgin. You see? If a girl don't go with a man she is always a virgin. In the country the girl never touches a man until her father has been paid in return. It's a bad habit. I don't know why... it's from a long way back. And they still hang on to it, I don't know why. If someone says:

    'I don't want to circumcise my daughter'

    they are frightened and neighbours will say: 'Oh, her daughter has still haram with her'.

    Haram means not been done, not pure. And also they are frightened of the 'yab, yab, yab'. Many women I know don't like it but nobody will marry the girl unless she is 'done' (circumcised) in my country. I was born in Ethiopia between Jejega and Dagga Bur. My country is Ethiopia. Ethiopians don't do it. I am Somali, I have never heard of Ethiopians doing it. May be Eritreans".

4. "Circumcision is looked forward to by the girls. It means 'make clean', purify. To her there aren't many things a girl can do. Besides the educated ... and even they are only in secondary roles. For a girl is motherhood and marriage. She

can only be married if she is circumcised. So she look forward to it. It is painful but the myths make it something to look forward to, then she goes through with it".

5. "I think they won't tell us why, but when I grew up I put two and two together".

6. "It is a strange thing you know, the divorce rate is high in Somalia. The emphasis is placed on chastity and virginity. A woman has to be circumcised or infibulated so that when she marries , her future husband, or rather her in laws can check she is a virgin and she must be circumcised to prove it. Virginity is paramount. And yet in Somalia, as well as here amongst the Somali community, the divorce rate is high. What's the point then? Why the emphasis on virginity when divorce is going to take place, when he is going to divorce and marry another woman? If the woman marries several times why this emphasis'.

7. "I think it is done because of the jealousy of men. They use religion to impose this practice, to cover man's jealousy to keep woman a virgin"

3. HABITS, TRADITION, RELIGION

Under this heading are incorporated many emotive statements from the women interviewed. Some of the feelings behind their experiences still reflect the larger notion of control of women and their sexual life, just as in Chapter 2, although this time it seems disguised under different cultural categories. The link to women's oppression is fundamental to the understanding of female circumcision as practice, ritual, and ultimately, way of life.

Some of the things raised are self-explanatory, others are embedded in the cultural framework of the countries concerned: they are about influences of traditions, the network of beliefs from which women draw support and comfort; they are about compromises between contemporary knowledge regarding circumcision and 'supposedly' religious beliefs; about a habitual way of life which is difficult to break.

More problematic even is the central belief behind the performing of female circumcision , i.e. that it acts as a factor for social and political integration and cohesion for all members of society. In particular, is worth mentioning that it is also linked to polygamy and the latter is also believed to be a cohesive factor for all members of society, although the women interviewed about female circumcision seemed to think otherwise, in fact that polygamy is also another form of maintaining men in the dominant position in the societies concerned.

1. "In different parts of Kenya they do it in different ways. In some places women are circumcised just before marriage. The man has to be there and see the blood and everything. Then people give the woman money when she is done".

2. "When you are there it seems so natural. It is just what happens, it doesn't seem so strange. When you are here though and you talk about it, it seems a problem. It seems more strange".

3. "Well I don't know how you call this, but our mothers, grand-mothers, their mothers' mothers did it".

4. "It is not in Islam. It is not in the Koran. It has nothing to with Islam".

5. "Religion gave the patriarchal society the excuse it needed It suited their ideals. In Arabia women are veiled and restricted. Circumcision is just another facet of that oppression".

6. "We now know that it is not a religious thing. But we are still doing it wherever we are. The reason we are doing it is not because we believe but because people say so. People come to my house and say that my girls have to be done. It is our custom and religion. There are many people who believe very strongly. Myself I feel very different. The more I think about it the worse I feel, but I would still do it to my daughters, because it is the belief of a lot of people".

7. "In my opinion people should stop the practice. But I know that in my country it will take a long time to stop. In Europe women should stop doing it".

8. "There is no control on men, they are free. Men can have four wives. But my daughter will be the only wife".

9. "I think it is carried out (female circumcision) mainly for cultural reasons".

4. HOW IS DONE, WHAT AGE AND FORM

It is widely known to people working in the field that in many countries of the western world, Britain, France, Sweden and to a lesser extent Canada and Australia, all countries which have a large immigrant population from Africa and the Middle East, female circumcision is still carried out. Circumcision is now performed in two ways: either the operation is done in private clinics for the more wealthy sections of these communities or the other way has involved parents taking their children back to their countries of origins or other countries where the practice is performed.

At this stage it is worth mentioning about the role of these traditional circumcisers. The latter were traditionally * part of a secret society (the headwoman and her assistants) and circumcision was the passage into womanhood. It was achieved through a dual stage: the initiation and the graduation ceremony. (1) Today, however, this is gradually disappearing and girls are circumcised at a younger and younger age, therefore what we could call a 'rite of passage' practiced in many different forms by different societies is less and less a ground for justification of such practices.

Perhaps as the report from the Minority Rights Group (2) pointed out, we need not worry about the livelyhood of these traditional circumcisers since they don't live by circumcising girls alone, but mostly by circumcising boys (a less controversial practice), birth attendances and other activities seem to supplement their income as well, such as: barber trade, farming, traditional healing, etc.

Here are some testimonies of how and when it takes place as well as who performs it and in what form.

1. "I was about ten years old, maybe even younger, then my mother and a lady came and they said they are going 'to make circumcision'. I was shocked, I thought I was going to die. Then I said:
   'Mama make me (go) first'

There were eight girls and I said make me the first one.

I don't want to hear all cry, and they hide. They took drum and they beat that drum when the girl is crying so as to cover up the crying. They chase the men away first of all and they beat the drum so the man doesn't hear.

'Make me first, make me first'

And she said ok and I was first".

2. "I don't remember much , I was only six. It was after my father died. It is less painful at that age".

3. "When they cut, they cut both sides. Then they put thorns, three thorns, then it closes. They don't give you any of the anaesthetic things to make you sleep. I can 'hear' the thorns going in still. Believe me, it has never gone out of my mind".

4. "I was eleven years old when I was circumcised. At the time we were living in the 'interior'. There were no doctors or a city near. At times when the other girls were done (my sister and cousins) I used to wonder when I was going to be done, not knowing the difficulties of the pain. In our country there are special women who do it, with no medical provision or qualifications. You never know whether you are going to die or live. The only thing you know is that this thing has to be done to you like to everyone else. There is no way that you can escape, because it is custom that all the women have to be done. When my time came, my nerves went to pieces, I was very afraid. When I see these women sitting around with all the things prepared I fainted but there was no sympathy for me. I tried to run from this woman but I couldn't because there was this woman and another five as well. They put me in a white gown and told me to clean myself, then they came and held my legs, arms and body and pinned me down on the floor. The woman sat on a very low stool called 'Minchiris', then they sat me in one. I was screaming and all of them were holding me down, at that

time I wished I had never been born. Half way through it I fainted and I didn't know anything else. Later when I woke up my legs were tied and I was lying on the floor; that lasted for seven days: not getting up and walking but sitting very still. After seven days the woman came back to look at it, to see if everything was well, luckily I was.

Then she took out the thorns which had been holding it together; some women are unlucky and have to be done again, but I was lucky, I was ok. After that I thought all my problems were over, but I was married when I was sixteen years old and I had the same difficulties because they had to open me up, there was no anaesthetic and it was the same kind of pain as when I was eleven, except even worse. Then it was the same all over again when I had my first child".

5. "It's done when girls are babies, two to three months old even".

6. "The men enjoy themselves, they don't get the pain, it's the women who suffer. The women have to stand up and stop the girls suffering because the child doesn't want to be done, it's old ladies that are doing it , somebody has to stop the old ladies. How come a woman becomes the one who does it? Everything has a background, they used to do it always, then they teach others. It's from always, she is called a "midgan" in Somalia, they know how to do it...they keep the knife clean, they clean it well".

7. "I was ten years old, a 'professional' woman does this sort of things. I grew up with my mother and grandmother because my father was away a lot. I was living in the 'interior', I always knew that one day this would happen to me. Because all the young children in my village had been done. One day my grandmother called this woman to our village. She came in the evening and stayed the night and I was afraid of what she was going to do to me. A lot of the little girls were afraid. I slept very little that night. In the morning I saw

the women out collecting the thorns, and then I knew my time had come. In the early morning I went out with the goats as usual but then I was called back. My mother told me to go and wash. Although I knew about it and it's traditional and everything, I was very frightened. My skin was 'crumpling'. Always my grandmother told me that it is very bad if you cry when it is being done, because it is something for every woman. Then all morning I had to stay with my mother and grandmother waiting, then it was done. All these women held me and I was crying".

5. HOW TO STOP IT

In 1985 a Bill was introduced in this country to prohibit female circumcision. Formal legislation, as often is the case, had not taken into consideration that without the appropriate links and consultation with the communities concerned and organisations like ourselves, it would only drive the practice underground.

The Bill was not accompanied by a programme of health and sex education to be implemented in an interim period, to counteract the consequences of making it illegal and a criminal act, given that certain sections of the communities in Britain which still practice it consider it an integral aspect of the their cultural life.

Although not opposed to the bill in theory, we have always felt, ever since its introduction that there was an implicit racism in a piece of legislation which prohibits the circumcision practice on 'custom and ritual' grounds and yet doesn't for reasons of 'physical and mental health' (3), a view which we have made known at the time through various articles and publicity. Basically white women may undergo surgery on grounds of (mental) health whilst the same standards are not applied to black women who may also feel that their well-being (mental and physical) is linked to the practice of circumcision, but for black women it would be classified under 'custom and ritual'.

What seems important is that the abolition of circumcision is not so much a matter of legislation, in fact to achieve eradication, I should be able to bring it out more and more in the open, something that this bill has not contributed to. As it has been shown even in the countries where circumcision is a widespread practice and where legislation was introduced as long ago as 1946 (Sudan) to prohibit the worst kind of mutilation: infibulation, it has not worked. A fairly recent study (1979) shows that 80% of Sudanese women continue to be infibulated. (4)

Below, always in our vein of first hand accounts, are four different experiences and feelings on whether and how to stop it:

1. "I think the best thing is if women come together and discuss it, and say what's good about it, why we do it if it's not religion".

2. "I want to help other people to stop, we have to talk to them, there is nothing else we can do: to our neighbour, to anyone that has a daughter, we have to talk to that lady with her daughter listening, then let the child have the fear a little bit and say:

   'No, don't do it to me mama'

   There is nothing else to do, we have to talk, we have to help the girl because it is her mum who is in charge. Spread the idea".

3. "They think maybe it's good. There is something that makes them frightened. It's background. Something says all the time: your child has not been done. If you are outside the country you should now be able to let your girl child free. They shouldn't do it. They are stupid to still do these things. The younger generations even do it. It's because their mothers tell them always. It's hard to stop. But keep talking and talking, keep going and going, tell them to stop. Some of them may chase you, but go on".

4. "I was born in Kenya. They do it there, not the pharaonic, the intermediate and excision. I was the fourth child. Mum is interested to do anything to help. I will be prepared to talk about it, and mum. We want to do anything to help people stop. I feel sorry"

6. COUNTERACTING THE IMAGES AND MYTHS

We are all familiar as women with the difficulties we encounter on a daily basis when we try to assert and re-claim our rights and although some things have improved in the last twenty years in terms of employment, education and health access, we still have a long way to go in terms of 'counteracting the image' of what women are in the eyes of men and the societal powers which on the whole they control still.

In recent years many black women have been instrumental in denouncing the dual ground of oppression that effects them in particular as well as share wherever possible the common platform with white women.

One of the most oppressing forms still in existence today which effect black women is the practice of female circumcision, the latter will never be understood, let alone eradicated, without the active help of many forces in society, from women's groups to women's health projects like the LBWHAP, and broad political progressive forces at large. One of the first steps that has and is been taken, is to counteract the positive image that female circumcision holds in the societies and communities that practice it.

The problem cannot be treated as a mere health issue, clearly medical research that shows the damage level suffered by women who undergo genital mutilation may be helpful towards discouraging and eradicating the practice, but it is equally important, if not more so, to aknowledge the social pressures which force women to do the operation.

The most emphatic of these pressures is marriage: for many women the latter is the only mean to achieve a minimum of economic security and this argument is valid not only for women in the 'underdeveloped' countries where the mutilation is practiced but also for women of those same societies who have moved to Britain, and for their daughters too: the problems encountered in this society still have produced the same results as in the so called 'underdeveloped countries', because language barriers, sexist and racist attitudes in particular have forfeited many attempts to achieve economic independence thereby eliminating the need to marry and to be circumcised as a consequence.

Other factors are involved however: the necessity to conform to one's society or community (as in the case of the communities in Tower Hamlet), even if they are male-dominated and full of restrictive practices and rules as regards women's behaviour.

Secondly, virginity (as mentioned before in this booklet) as a prerequisite to marriage and the former (need to conform) are completely bound up with the practice of genital mutilation, virginity for the cultures who practice the latter, means being sown up, it has nothing to do with the hymen and being a virgin inside. However, as one of the women's accounts will explain, being mutilated and sown up is not necessarily a safeguard, i.e. circumcision is not necessarily a safeguard for virginity and in some cases it can also be the cause of misunderstanding and suffering, as in the case outlined below.

Only recently the LBWHAP was asked help and support by a young woman who for the reasons mentioned above was literally divorced the next morning after the marriage, the distress however had come from the fact that this young woman was indeed a virgin since she had never had intercourse before marriage and was no longer a virgin only in so far as she was unstitched, which had happened as a result of side effects from the operation itself. Another example of how being a virgin and female genital mutilation, and being sown up don't really bear any relation to one another.

Lastly a further pressure is created by the cultural notion of cleanliness and aesthetic: the idea of the female genitals as being dirty and ugly (a notion that exist also in our own society, although we don't cut them off). Another notion which is widespread in societies practicing female circumcision is that the clitoris is dangerous during childbirth, being an aggressive, male organ. (5)

As I can see from this enlistment there are a lot of images and myhts to obliterate in order to change beliefs and practices bound up with the performing of female circumcision. However to end this section on a positive note, many things have changed for many women in Britain, and not for them alone. For example, for many women in parts of Eritrea, marriage patterns are changing, for example arranged marriages are less frequent (also connected with female circumcision), people choose their own partners, education has changed people's attitudes. In Eritrea up to 80% of the population no longer practice female circumcision.

1. "People think that if a girl is sewn she can't be doing anything. But it is not so. She can be doing things whether she is sewn or not. They think it a safe thing to do, but it is not. It is barbaric and butchering. Many women could talk to the girls and educate them. The girls have to know that they are not safe sown. I do not agree with women taking girls to Arabia and to Somalia to be done. I don't have any children though, so no one take any notice of me. They say it is healthy to do it. How can it be healthy to cut bits off? It's more healthy not to cut our bodies. They should leave us as God made us".

2. "In the past a woman had to prove she was a virgin before a marriage took place. A discussion took place to make sure that she had remained a virgin, by the way she had led her life. If there was any suspicion then there was a check by the family. But this happened a long time ago".

3. "One of the reasons I left Somalia with three small children travelling across fourteen hundred miles of arid parched country was the discovery that my husband planned to do a pharaonic circumcision, a complete circumcision".

4. "When I was about fifteen I had three big brothers who were all looking for a nice girl to marry and they want a lot of money for her. They want to give me a man to marry... they were waiting for me to listen to them. They gave me a man and I didn't like him ... I run away at the time the Italians were in Ethiopia, it was their last year before the British came. This one Italian had been three years in the country... I ran away and married this Italian soldier from a Somali father. They had to return all the animals and three guns and two

horses. They had a lot of things and they had to return them all. I said I didn't want that man, I didn't want him, so they had to give it all back. I said, too bad, and ran away. They didn't get anything, they were very cross. Because of that I will never go back. To this day I have never been back to my village. To jejega yes".

5. "They still see it as an essential part of socialisation in Somali culture. They just don't see it as a problem. It is a problem. It causes pain, it is debilitating. One woman I talked to was for it. But by the end you could see that she saw the contradictions. She said if I had an education like you I would be against it, but I don't have an education. I can't get a job so I have to comply, meaning 'if I wasn't dependent, if I could support myself, I would'. I 'need' to belong to my community".

6. "I knew that I was going to get married, but I didn't know when. In our country you don't have boyfriends, you don't have if you are a girl. You can't say 'I want to marry Abdulla'. A man decides who he wants to marry and he asks the family. Then your family might ask you or they simply say yes or no to him. They want you to have a husband who can look after you well".

7. "I was about seven years old, I was feeling great, because if I wouldn't have been done, they would have called me names (for example buryo qab) meaning impure and unclean. From the day you have this operation and get rid off that piece of flesh, you consider yourself mature and responsible.

And all the little girls in the village look forward to that big day. We were living in a small village in the North, my father was 'aqil', head of a tribe. I never forgot such a torture and painful operation. My mother was away on that particular day, I asked Sharifo, our neighbour to include me with the group, when I found out that she called the midwife to circumcise her three daughters. I was so delighted when she agreed. The next morning we were told to clean up ourselves and the lady came in carrying her tools".

7. WHOSE DECISION?

Even in contemporary times the decision whether a girl should be circumcised or not rests on the whole with the family. With the exception of Eritrea, as mentioned earlier, where an education programme has been implemented to stop the practice in the last twenty five years (see Appendix 1) and which has been quite successful, although at times it has been replaced with a less drastic form: the 'sunna'. In other cases (like in Sudan) legislation has made infibulation illegal but not excision thus only allowing for the partial improvement of the situation.

The older generation are also still in favour of the practice and will take the decison to have it performed on their grandchildren or in some cases even perform it themselves, if their own sons and daughters will refuse to do so.

In some other cases it isn't even a conscious decision, it's just done without either discussion or consultation. These decisions and whoever make them are backed up by tenacious beliefs, we could say that it is a tacit social decision in many ways, and it is certainly considered one of the many aspects of the cultural infrastructure.

For example in many areas it is part and parcel of a larger process of a systematic and lengthy training of girls 'to take their place' in the community, although that is less and less the case nowadays. There is a great difficulty in removing the decision either from parents, grandparents, mothers and grandmothers or any other relation and superimpose the decision of the host culture either through the use of the legislation available and professional bodies concerned, many a time the labels adopted for female circumcision are wholly inappropriate: the most common one being child abuse. However, other avenues have been explored besides the most central one of working with the women themselves who have been circumcised, and they have been mainly to get all members of the community involved in discussing it and bringing it out in the open, particularly with influential religious leaders.

Another important obstacle is the belief that some black women still hold, they claim that it is a question of solidarity, that female circumcision (unlike what we term clitoridectomy, as performed in modern western medicine) creates a bond between women, it is performed by women on women, thus retaining the cohesion of the female role within the tribe or ethnic group. (6)

Conflicts over circumcision can arise between different members of a family, between husband and wife. As it is stated in one of our testimonies some women from the Somali community in East London are separated, and although there are other reasons like equality within the home and the realisation that it is no longer necessary for a woman to be treated like a 'chair' in order for her to survive, as it is no longer necessary to be circumcised in order to be married or for women to survive economically, ultimately the economic power which had always been in the hands of the 'husband' is no longer central to the economics of the family or of society in general. (For example over 50% of the female population in Britain works outside the home).

Male power groups within society have not however completely disappeared, whether they may be elders or mere traditionalists, and are still struggling to maintain the status quo, so that some of the fundamental cornerstones of dominance: reproduction and servicing as the role of women may go unchanged.

Ther real problem is how to maintain certain traditions and rituals which are positive and central to all the community and eliminate others which are harmful: to make the people behind the 'decision' need not fear the loss altogether of their roots, culture, but just accept recognition of the harmful aspects. Certainly a comparative tool (a study which is being undertaken at the moment) could be useful at least to point out that in nearly all societies as far as women are concerned some harmful practices were and are undertaken, even in the so called civilised societies.

1. "I think it is a bad thing really. Both my daughters were done. It was my family's will. It was just done somehow.

    No dicussion. It just is".

2. "No, my husband says no. He thinks it is bad. People don't do it now (?). In Sudan if you want it done and you go to the doctors they refuse to do it. If a midwife does it she will be in trouble with the doctors and get no more work".

3. "My father died and people kept telling my mother that I should be done as early as possible, because I was an orphan".

4. "I was 11 years old when I was circumcised, my grandmother did the operation while my mother was away. My mother arrived two days afterwards. It was the pharaonic type".

5. 'Well, I think it is necessary to do a little bit. I agree with sunna but not the pharaonic type of circumcision.

8. PHYSICAL, SEXUAL AND PSYCHOLOGICAL DAMAGE

The physical consequences are more self-evident and in many ways better known than the psychological or sexual problems which arise out of infibulation and excision. Physical damage is usually extensive and long-lasting, to put it in the words of one of the women who suffered mutilation: 'It is a problem as long as you live'.

Physical damage is considered on two levels and certainly felt by women in the same way. The immediate usually entails haemorrage, cut of other organs (the bladder, the urethra, vaginal walls, etc.) if the young girl, child struggles a lot during the performance of the operation. Infection can also result from poor hygienic conditions. We must not assume that these conditions are usually associated with the countries who practice it, given the secrecy that the legislation of 1985 has created, it would be very difficult to establish how much the practice is undertaken in this country under the same or similar conditions, even if we are not talking of a large number of women, it is not at all sure that it is not happening at all.

The long term damage is even more extensive as it effects a greater number of women and at different stages in their lives: during puberty, sexual maturity, during childbirth, etc. When menstruating many women suffer dysmennorhea (painful menstruations) since the opening is usually too small for the blood to flow out. Urinating also is sometime difficult and infection of both the uterus and the bladder also results from accumulation of poison inside the body. There are also side effects in terms of various formations which have been found in mutilated women like cysts, scars, etc.

Complications and damage are unavoidable both during sexual intercourse and childbirth: in the former severe pain (dyspaurenia) and little or no enjoyment may be the result of the mutilation. In the MRG report it is stated that even the less harmful of clitoridectomy (like the sunna) entails the removal of nerves vital to the process of enjoyment and orgasming and works are quoted to back such statement (7). I would like to take issue with this view, because the women both interviewed by the project (LBWHAP) and members of the latter sustain that there is not a total removal of pleasure and that the nerve system that relates to orgasm still exists after amputation.

More importantly, what at times is believed to be solely a result of circumcision, is in fact a combination of factors, one in particular relates to the lack of interest in their partners by women who never chose them, and the position they hold within a polygamous marriage. That is not to belittle the gravity of female mutilation in any way, but to understand it in its complete cultural context so that eradication may be the more successful.

Some studies have tried to establish whether man get satisfaction having intercourse with infibulated/excised women; however we feel this is not perhaps as important an issue in question as the position of women, even if clearly a case could be made that given that enough men still support the practice, if they were brought to confront their own sexual practices and related enjoyment, (after all one of the central beliefs is that circumcised women are clean and more sexy circumcised), it may make a large contribution towards the eradication of female genitals mutilation.

For example, as part of the study done in Sierra Leone by Olayinka Koso-Thomas (8) in attitudes towards female circumcision, out of fifteen men ten stated that they preferred uncircumcised women, as they felt that the response from the latter to sexual intercourse was more shared in terms of enjoyment.

During childbirth infibulated women have to be cut in order for them to have the child. Foetal death and brain damage have been known to be side effects of protracted and obstructed labour. Episiotomy (caeserean) is adopted as a matter of course which can also cause damage to the child and mother. And of course the mothers who have normal births may be resewn, as custom demands, only to be reopened if she has another baby.

To many of the women which have been in contact with the LBWHAP this had happened more than once since having just one child is not accepted on the whole and is certainly not part of the custom, in fact we could safely say that most societies internationally, with the exception of the last thirty years in the advanced industrialised countries and only for certain groups and class within them, have always expected women to have many children.

Infection caused by the mutilations sometime ascend to the reproductive organs thus sometime causing sterility.

The problems connected with female circumcision are truly immense and painful, the medical specific list of side effects and consequences is truly a long one. We just restrict ourselves here in mentioning the side effects not using the specific technical language of medicine, as that it is not really our purpose here but just to tell the story of the 'pain' at whatever level it is lived, the case is always better stated by the women who suffered the consequences:

"It is the cutting up of part of our bodies, you are talkin' about".

I briefly mention the psychological effects, briefly not because they are less important or less frequent but because we know as yet very little about the psychological side-effects of these mutilations. Very little research has yet been done on the subject and not so much has transpired from the contact with women in London. The very nature of the subject doesn't allow much insight since female circumcision has always been shrouded in secrecy.

However I do have some personal accounts and testimonies and I shall record them in full later, even if they only 'state' the silence on the subject, (which is in itself a sign of psychological trauma) some women are not shouting, not crying out, they are crying within, in silent tears. Clearly the trauma is lived for some women before, during and after the operation, the fear and pain sometime lived at such an early age, and particularly the sense of estrangement and humiliation that ensue after the mutilation. There have also been cases of women who don't have children as a result of female circumcision, not because of any physical damage, as mentioned earlier in this chapter, but because of the psychological stress.

There are arguments which sustain that psychological side effects as I understand them are not so much applicable for example in the case of societies where to be circumcised is part of the norm, even to be accompanied by festivities, presents, a sense of having passed from childhood world into womanhood and responsibility. And where if one is not circumcised one is considerd dirty, impure, so that perhaps the psychological side-effects would stem from not being circumcised and not vice-versa: with problems of non-identification, of feeling different. Psychological side-effects more likely to manifest themselves in the case of not being mutilated.

The western world has a tendency to see and apply western sciences, like psychology (and psychiatry), in this case, notion's of mental ilness which stem from itself rather than look at the appplicability of such notion in other types of societies.

However it would be useful to see through new research and studies whether the cultural framework that supports genital mutilation for women is still strong enough to continue support such a painful practice; that does not seem to be the case in London so much. And if despite all support and ideological concepts backing it of the nature mentioned earlier, whether young girls and women still suffer at an internal level, perhaps even unknown to the societies and communities concerned is something that needs to be looked at on the grounds of that culture's beliefs and practices.

1. "Circumcision is horrible, really bad, you have to be cut every time you have children. Both sides six times, I nearly died

once with a big baby: there was no midwife".

2. "When you are young you get cut. Then you are married and you are cut open again. It causes other difficulties in this country (Britain) because when you are having a baby they look at you and they immediately put you for caeserean section. When they see a woman that has been cut they immediately assume that she is not normal. Also we have periods difficulties. Most women complain of this. Although it is a tradition, I think it should stop".

3. "I had so many difficulties afterwards. Then I was strapped up for seven days. I bled a lot and was weak for many months. These difficulties stay with you always. For me not so much as some women because I never had children, because I was always worried about these things and had a lot of problems in there, with my periods, my back and everything. Maybe that is why I never had children. It was very bad".

4. "I was in bed for one week and then I was ok. When I married I had to be cut, it had to be done. It was very painful".

5. " I think I wouldn't do it to my daughter. When I came through, it was really hard, because I had to have it done twice, and then I was married: I had to be opened, and for as long as you live you'll have that problem. So I won't do it. And a lot of Somali people are thinking of not doing it".

6. "I remember when I saw the knife I did not know where I remember one leg here and the other here (spread open), a lady holding each one and me screaming, just screaming then I don't remember anything until it's finished. Then I lay on the bed for seven days and they tie me with straps around my legs, but they clean it always, they bring salt water, it burns so hot. They put salt in warm water and they clean from both sides two times a day for seven days. Then they open three of the strings they tie me with. There was one

left around the very top of my legs, which was on for two weeks. I used to walk a little bit and I have got a bit better. After six weeks it was all stuck together. I couldn't make a wee because it was all stuck together".

7. "I remained in bed for several days. I was not allowed to intake fluids in order not to pass water frequently. I was not able to walk. About seven days or so later, the "operator" came again with her instruments to check if the operation was successful, and approved that it was well done. From that day I was allowed to walk but slowly with the support of a stick and eat and drink according to my wish".

8. "When I have my first baby they cut and every time I have a child they cut again. All of the stiching makes it small so they have to cut it. I was tied up for eight days, I mustn't move. I mustn't drink water or anything else that would make me pass urine. It was really bad to pass urine".

9. "After seven days, they want to do the work again. They wanted to open it again. Three women hold me and they bring scissors. And they started to cut me, it was painful, no anaesthetic. I had shock, I started to shake, for seven days I was feeling bad hardly able to pass urine. I think the younger people are more brave. I couldn't take it if they did it today".

10. "I don't remember a lot, it was very painful. But a funny thing happened at the time. On the third day after my operation I was still tied up - my legs were bound together. Everyone was out looking after the goats and so on. I was in a building without doors and alone when a thief came to steal. I was frightened, firstly of opening my wound and bleeding and secondly of the intruder. He threatened me to show him were all the valuables were. I told him I could not move, but I pointed out things to him. He took what he could and he ran away. My mother was grateful I was allright".

11. "I don't want to talk about this (sex and sexuality). We don't talk about these things. It was very bad. People would not understand. Nobody talks about these things. I always had problems with my blood and things. Nobody thinks it is connected to the circumcision. I was very frightened when it was done and have always had problems and fear".

CONCLUSION

There is no conclusion to be had with something like female circumcision until the far off day when it will be completetely eradicated. In the meanwhile the struggle to combat it through counselling, advice, education and support and the knowledge that this may bring comfort to at least a few women who have undergone mutilation and perhaps stop a few more young girls and women to 'go under the knife' is enough to give us strength to continue the work for eradication.

Dealing with the health issues that effect black women in terms of female circumcision (as well as others) is an important and central part of the LBWHAP's project.

Circumcision, mutilation of women's genitals is a harmful practice, as you have read from the many first hand accounts it causes pain, problems and restricts black women emotionally and sexually. Whatever the reasons behind it and as we have seen they are many, it is just another example of the universal oppression of women. It is also true that it is easy for the West to criticise the 'third world' and its harmful practices, but if we never lose sight of its political context, the oppression of black women could be a pivotal point towards the challenging of all oppressions.

Progress has been made in the implementation of education and support programmes in many countries: Senegal, Somalia, Sudan, Egypt, Kenya etc, as well as in Britain (and other western countries where it is practiced) with projects like ourselves and FORWARD (Foundation For Women's Health Research And Development) which deals with work both here and internationally. The other organisation it's worth mentioning once again, the Inter-African Committee (IAC), set up in 1984 which is concerned specifically with 'traditional practices affecting the health of women and children in Africa', where female circumcision is but one and the United Nations, World Health Organisation.

The cultural pressures to conform and continue the practice of female mutilation is also reinforced by racist attitudes in this country, as ethnic groups feel threatened by dominant ideology: attempts to stamp out the practice is often understood (and perhaps that's indeed the intention, for example behind the Circumcision Act of 1985) as a design to undermine traditional values. One way, as somebody suggested, towards helping the eradication would be to change the practice by persuading 'traditional operators' to transform the operation to a symbolic cut which would establish the objective to stop the operation and on the other hand maintain the ceremonial aspects.

This booklet is another attempt, amongst many to raise the issues of the consequences of female circumcision, the long process of education and raising awareness is undoubtedly an effective one, but the abolition of this practice needs also a strong political will and concerted effort at local and governmental level (as well as links and co-ordination at an international level), particularly in terms of direct support, such as financing of health and educational projects throughout the country where communities that undertake the practice live.

APPENDIX 1

Interview with the representative of the National Union of Eritrean Women

Q. Is the practice of female circumcision practiced in Eritrea?

A. It is not so widespread anymore, but it used to be.

Q. What type of female circumcision is practiced?

A. The partial removal of the clitoris - we call it 'Menkenshab' suna.

Q. Who normally performs the operation?

A. A woman in the community - but not a relative.

Q. Are you circumcised?

A. Yes

Q. Would you circumcise your baby daughter?

A. Definitely not. It is no longer seen as necessary.

Q. How has this change in attitudes occured?

A. Well, you have to understand the political situation in Eritrea. As you may be aware we have been fighting for independence from Ethiopia for many years. The Eritrean People's Front has been fighting for twenty-five years now. Eritrea is split in two, the People's Front are active in one half. An education programme has been in progress since then to stop practices like female circumcision. The education programme went from village to village explaining the harmful effects on the body from genital mutilation.

Q. Do you think that the state of war and political situation has helped in the change of attitudes?

A. Definitely. It is a difficult situation to live in. Always in danger and not knowing the future. So cultural practices have had to change. But the Eritrean People's Front have introduced a systematic form of education too. Women's organisations like ours have also taken up the campaign, ours is ten years old, in the UK things have just started. (Referring to the LBWHAP - interview undertaken in 1986)

APPENDIX 2

Complete Interview with Layla

Q. How long have you been with the Somali people?

A. Thirty-four years, since I was sixteen, when I married Ismal. I have been married nearly thirty years.

Q. Have you been to Somalia since then?

A. Yes, twice.

Q. I believe your first daughter was circumcised?

A. Yes. First can I just say that although I am an English woman, I am speaking as a Somali woman. I just want to make that clear... I know that the British government is trying to ban circumcision (this interview was recorded just before the Circumcision Act of 1985 was passed) and I am very much against that.

Q. Why?

A. Because I don't think that it is up to the government to decide what ethnic minorities should or shouldn't be doing. They should investigate before they make any drastic decisions. I don't think the government knows what it is doing to people and families in this country.

Q. Can you tell me about your daughter, and your time in Somalia, and what was happening there?

A. My daughter was circumcised in Somalia, in a hospital. She had anaesthetic, so she didn't know anything of what was happening. She didn't know what had been taken away, or any illness it would cause her. All she knew was that she was closely closed up. I discussed it with her only when she was going to get married.

But when she was a child I used to always notice her knickers... with urine and blood stains. And I used to say to her to clean up, and she said she did, she had problems weeing and had difficult periods. it was only when she married that I realised what this thing meant. She was shivering from head to foot, we couldn't control her.

Q. Did they give her an anaesthetic to open her?

A. Well, no. We brought a Somali woman from Liverpool. She was once a nurse..and she used to do these things. But even the way they open her, with .. a stick, they put it in the hole, pull it up, stretch the skin and then cut it with a razor.

Q. Do you think it is clever in a way?

A. Yes, it is, but you can't get a straight cut, you have to do it bit by bit. Each cut was a knife in my back. But she only opened her a little, because she couldn't take anymore. When she was married she had a lot of problems with penetration. I think it was then that she turned her back on her family. Because of the thing that was done to her, and because my other two girls weren't circumcised, she felt that there was something wrong with her. The reason why she was circumcised was never discussed. She divorced her husband after three months, which took seven years. She says to me that at that time she didn't think anyhting was wrong. She had never discussed women's private parts with anybody else, so she didn't know any different.

Q. Did she discuss it with Somali women?

A. No. She neither discussed it with Somali or English women. I don't think Somali people like to do that anyway. Although she is married now, I don't get much feedback she is shy to talk about it. I know that her sexual life is not right. And she was also very badly stitched, inside and outside, after the baby was born.

Q. How do your other two daughters who have not been circumcised feel about it, given that it is a very Somali family?

A. Well, they believe that it shouldn't be done at all. They have now come to the decision that it is no longer needed. Because men before were like animals and just used to jump on anybody, but now they are more educated.

Q. Do your daughters worry that they won't get married because they aren't circumcised?

A. I have five sons and only one of them wants a woman who is circumcised. Because he feel he would be missing out on something.

Q. What about your husband?

A. You can't teach an old dog new tricks, you can try and talk him out of it, but if it came to a decision he would want it.

Q. What is your opinion of what you saw happening in Somalia?

A. I have seen girls circumcised and it was like branding cattle. No men are allowed in the area. It's a man made thing. I believe it's a man made thing. They can kill something but they don't want to watch this. They would fasten her legs with rope and they would stitch her with thorns. Afterwards, the legs are fastened from the hips to the ankles. They stay like that for days. They just leave her like a dying animal. She is just left to rot, they just feed her. She is not changed, she is not washed. After several days when she is bathed, that's when the agony starts. That's the only thing I don't agree with in Somalia.

Q. How do you think this thing will stop at grass roots level?

A. By bringing people together to discuss it and to vote... to talk about it. Most people don't realise what it is all about. All of my girls are educated sexwise now, my daughters are free as birds, I give them their freedom because they have had sex education. They know that men are animals, that's all they want. Women should know more about sexual satisfaction, and their sexual life.

Q. In the Somali tradition and community women never talk about sex at all. We want to talk about female circumcision and all these things. How do we begin to do this?

A. Look at how many divorced women there are in the Somali community. What is the reason for them being divorced? Is it sexual? Money? Don't they like the man? Is there any or no sexual life? Women have got to start to talk.

Q. I put an article in the newspaper about stopping female circumcision. People in the community went mad, they said it was a bad thing to do. What do you think?

A. We need to have meetings. Speak regularly and freely.

Q. You have two daughters who are not circumcised? Why didn't you do them?

A. Because of my eldest daughter and what she went through. No way would I allow the others to be done. Any man who says I won't marry your daughter because she is not circumcised doesn't have any real feelings about her in the first place. She is who she is, whether she is circumcised or not.

Q. ...your daughter who is circumcised, will she do her daughter?

A. No way.

Q. Does ... talk about these things?

A. Not much. What has been done has been done. She sees why it was done at the time. It wasn't this that was a problem in her marriage. I don't think Somalis marry for love anyway.

Q. What do they marry for?

A. It's the family. Everyone wants a good husband or wife for their children.

Q. In British and European culture there are things which the Somali people would be shocked about, eg facelifts. Would it help for Somalis to see these things?

A. Now that circumcision is becoming a public issue, women feel people are trespassing and interfering because it's about themselves, it's a private thing. They probably think that nothing happens to anyone else. Circumcision causes bad health, bad childbirth, bad sex. So it is not really a comparison, you get a facelift in order to better yourself. If women want satisfaction then they have to stop circumcision.

APPENDIX 3

Amina A. Ibrahim is the outreach/development worker of the LBWHAP. She has three daughters and she decided not to circumcise them. She supports and advocates openly the total eradication of female circumcision.

The paragraphs below are an extract from am interview with her, this is what she has to say about her decision:

"I decided not to circumcise my daughters because it is unnecessary and very painful. I don't want my children to go through what I have, I don't want to see them suffering physical and mental traumas that is caused by this horrific operation. It is not easy to break away from a deep rooted cultural tradition and all the pressures that go with it, but some people should start otherwise it will be like it is now forever.

A lot of people think it is embarassing to talk about female circumcision, even the women who have stopped circumcising their daughters are not coming forward to discuss with other women who might or might not be effected by the practice. I am not ashamed to talk about female circumcision and I am telling everybody that I am not circumcising my daughters. By the time my children are twenty the mothers of their peer group will regret that they have circumcised their children. Families should think about the future of their children and should not be dragged by an outdated custom or culture. It does not suit the children of today".

APPENDIX 4

This appendix was added later to this booklet, just before it was due to go to the printer and it is added as a result of the debate that has taken place at the first conference on Female Genital Mutilation (1 February 1989) taking place in this country and organised by FORWARD (Foundation for Women's Health Research and Development). The debate we are concerned with and which has always been at the forefront of the eradication campaign is one which establishes whether female genital mutilation constitutes child abuse or not.

In the list of recommendations that the conference agreed on is interesting to notice that although there was a general opinion regarding female genital mutilation constituting child abuse:

"Female genital mutilation constitutes child abuse. In this context however, it does not constitutes child sexual abuse" (Recommendation No. III)

There was also an awareness of the difference that the two entailed as well as the knowledge that although two very different things, their meaning can be easily interchanged and the terminology 'child abuse' carry on the whole very negative connotations:

"Although female genital mutilation does constitute child abuse, it was aknowledged that the label child abuse has unnecessary pejorative connotations and its use may be counterproductive" (Recommendation No. IV)

We would also like to acknowledge the first recommendation made at the conference regarding the term female circumcision, and although this booklet has been written prior to the conference and it makes use interchangeably of the two terms (genital mutilation and circumcision) we have always been aware that the terminology female circumcision is a rather euphemistic (and traditional) way of describing the practice, and that female genital mutilation may be more appropriate:

"The terminology female circumcision should be avoided and be replaced by the term: female genital mutilation". (Recommendation No. I)

Below is the paper presented at the conference, (subsequently incorporated in the Report published by FORWARD - see Bibliography for details) by the LBWHAP and which we reproduce below in order to reiterate the project's position regarding the fact that female circumcision does not constitute child abuse as such.. The position of the LBWHAP is not to belittle its gravity or diminish in any way the efforts towards eradication, but to understand the practice in terms of its cultural context.

DOES FEMALE CIRCUMCISION CONSTITUTE CHILD ABUSE?
by London Black Women's Health Action Project,
Bethnal Green, London.

The movement to eradicate female circumcision in Africa has met with formidable cultural resistance in those areas where it is practiced despite efforts of the United Nations, international, regional and national bodies.

Our project strongly believes that the practice which is so deeply rooted in millions of people's culture cannot be eradicated so quickly and also female circumcision must be understood and located in the overall context of black struggle. In this context, there are two main areas providing the framework:

1. To counter state control and repression and criminalisation of issues of female sexuality.

2. To counter the image of black people as either:
    a) Performing 'barbaric' primitive practices (including female circumcision).

    b) Or the opposite - do not touch the behaviour at all because it is culturally appropriate and specific. Social services should not be blocked in 'liberalism'.

Our project deals with the rights of a child and her protection. We believe that the female is nobody's protected property. We maintain that female circumcision does not constitute consistent and ongoing undermining of a child.

Our ultimate goal is that through education, eradication of this practice will be reached. We do not want these families to be alienated and labelled as child abusers therefore criminals. We know that the operation is felt to be an act of love, not cruelty.

These families already suffer from discrimination. A woman may still go home and despite being empowered by these ideals, tradition may prove stronger. Calling female circumcision child abuse and putting it in the same category as sexual child abuse is counter productive. It is not looked at from African perspective but from western viewpoint. Imposing a law cannot change anything as long as people want it (not a few people but the whole community). Means of by-passing the law is always available.

Total change of the consciousness of the people who practice female circumcision is essential. For this to occur co-operation of the people is needed. Anything that harms the relationship between the people and female circumcision eradication projects is not necessary.

APPENDIX 5

FEMALE CIRCUMCISION

POLICY IMPLICATIONS FOR
WELFARE DEPARTMENTS

A DISCUSSION PAPER PREPARED BY
THE SOUTH AUSTRALIAN
CHILDREN'S INTEREST BUREAU

Author: Sally N. Castell-McGregor,
          Executive Officer,
          Children's Interests Bureau,
          3rd Floor, Da Costa Building,
          68 Grenfell Street,
          ADELAIDE, S.A. 5000.

WHAT IS FEMALE CIRCUMCISION?

This is a general term used to describe various types of genital mutilation.

INTRODUCTION

An estimated seventy million women and female children are circumcised in one form or another with several thousand new operations performed each day.(1) The practice occurs in more than 20 African countries from the Atlantic to the Red Sea, the Indian Ocean and the Eastern Mediterranean. Outside Africa a severe form of circumcision is practised in Oman, South Yemen and in the United Arab Emirates and a milder form among Moslem populations of Malaysia and Indonesia. It is also practised amongst migrants from these countries to Britain and France and has been reported in Australia.

The severity of the mutilations varies from country to country. There are three different types of circumcision which are briefly described below:

1. **"Sunna" or "Traditional" Circumcision**

   This involves the removal of the tip or hood of the clitoris. This, the mildest form, affects only a small proportion of the millions of women concerned.

2. **Excision/Clitoridectomy**

   This involves the partial or total removal of the clitoris plus the removal of adjacent tissues - both lips of the vulva (labia minora) without actually closing the vulva.

3. **Infibulation or "Pharaonic" Circumcision**

   This is the most severe practice. It involves the complete removal of the clitoris and adjacent tissues (labia minora and often the whole of the labia majora). The two sides of the vulva are then "joined" together with catgut or thorns, leaving a small opening for menstrual flow and the passing of urine.

The age at which the practice occurs is becoming younger and has less and less to do with initiation into adulthood.(2) It is suspected that when legislation against the practice is foreseen mothers will arrange earlier circumcision before their daughters are old enough to protest. One Mali study showed that 99% of excisions occur before puberty and 53% before the age of one year.

THE IMPLICATIONS OF FEMALE CIRCUMCISION

These are both physical (including immediate reactions such as shock, haemorrhage, retention of urine; longer term uro-genital and pelvic infections caused by use of unsterile instruments and lack of adequate hygiene; retention of menstual blood; obstetric complications leading to a risk for mother and baby and possible infertility; painful intercourse). Psychological reactions are anxiety and terror about the operation. However, research as to the latter and sexual implications of the process is still scant.

REASONS FOR FEMALE CIRCUMCISION

The origins of female circumcision are obscure as is our knowledge about why the practice occurs in some cultures and not in others. Overall, female circumcision is seen by many as an attempt to repress female sexuality.

The Minority Rights Group Report on Female Circumcision referred to earlier, cites four commonly given reasons for female circumcision:

1. Religious

   FACT: There is no basis whatsoever in any religion for the practice of female circumcision and infibulation. There is no support for it in the "Koran" nor does it occur in Saudi Arabia, the cradle of Islam. Confusion about the religious interpretation is probably due to a generalisation from male circumcision to females. Dr. Taha Ba'asher, Regional Adviser on Mental Health for the World Health Organisation for the Western Mediterranean wrote:

"While there is a general concensus of opinion that circumcision was one of the commands, when the Lord made trial of the Prophet Abraham, there is no clear indication in the case of female circumcision."

2. Sexual

Among some of the "sexual" reasons for female circumcision are:

attenuation of sexual desire (presence of the clitoris is thought by some to result in excessive sexual appetite), (uncircumcised women among the Bororos tribe in Sudan are called "bush bitches")(3);

- protection of female goat-herds from rape;

- protection of females from their own sexual desires;

- preservation of virginity in cultures where this is an absolute pre-requisite for marriage;

- an "hermaphroditic" view of human beings as possessing male and female and the need therefore to "remove" the "masculine" element (clitoris) in a girl and the feminine (foreskin) in a boy;

- a fear in some African countries that the clitoris is dangerous to the man and the baby during delivery.

CULTURAL

Female circumcision is seen by some as part of initiation into adulthood with the attendant ceremonies. However, this is queried by one (unpublished) thesis based on a study of practice in Mali. The author's respondents cited hygiene (32% - male and female), custom (23%) and no explanation (23%) as the reasons for excision. On a practical note bride-price cannot be obtained if a girl is not a virgin.

FEMALE CIRCUMCICISON
AS A CHILDREN'S RIGHTS ISSUE

Apart from the equally serious issues that this practice raises - the subjugation of women, women's health and the problems of poverty and under-development, female circumcision has to be seen as a serious infringement of children's rights. The child subjected to the process does not consent and is physically and traumatically assaulted. The practice is contrary to Article 5 of the Universal Declaration of Human Rights (that provision relating to the non-use of torture, cruel, unhuman or degrading treatment) and is contrary to the 1959 United Nations Declaration of Children's Rights.

These infringements are acknowledged by the Minority Rights Group (based in London) and many African women's groups vocal in their own countries and overseas. The international "voice" of children's rights, The Defence for Children International, has added its voice as an opponent to the practice which does not only occur in the countries already identified. In fact, reports of female genital mutilation have been reported in Britain, Sweden and France - all of which countries have large immigrant populations from Africa and the Middle East. Some of these involved "traditional" excisers being brought from the country of origin - others involve reports of the operation being done in private clinics for non-medical reasons.

FEMALE CIRCUMCISION IN AUSTRALIA

Extent and Medical Response

We do not know the extent to which circumcision of female children is practised in Australia. The Federal Department of Health has received representations about it from time to time but its attempts to elicit more detailed information from health authorities, general practitioners or interest groups have not been successful. The Federal Department sees the matter as relating largely to questions of child abuse and therefore one which comes under the ambit of the individual states. I am informed by Dr. Cathy Mead, Medical Services Adviser on Women's Health and

Family Planning, that as the people from the Cocos (Keeling) Islands constitute one of the community groups reputed to be engaged in the practice in Western Australia, the Department of Territories is pursuing the matter with the relevant Western Australian authorities. Much of our information concerning circumcision of female children is anecdotal and usually comes via media coverage.

The Australian Medical Association does not have a specific policy on female circumcision. However, the General Secretary of the Association advised me in a letter dated 30th September, 1986:

"While there may be occasional medical reasons for clitoridotomies, such as for malignant disease in older patients and on children with "inter-sex" problems associated with clitoral hypertrophy, there is, in the view of the Australian Medical Association, no place for ritual female circumcision - which really is of the nature of genital mutilation for traditional, non-medical reasons.

As far back as July 21st/August 2nd, 1980 the Federal Council of the Australian Medical Association resolved to advise the Director-General of Health that it condemns the practice."

The A.M.A. further supported the qualification of items in the Medical Benefits Schedule for the purpose of <u>male</u> circumcision by the inclusion of the words "where medically necessary". The Minister of Health, Dr. Blewett, reversed this in July, 1985 on the grounds that unavailability of a Medicare benefit might be an economic hardship and lead to "backyard" practices. The Minister concluded that the use of medical benefits schedule was not the best way to limit the practice - preferring education and informed discussion.(4) Benefits may be payable for "amputation of the clitoris where medically indicated" (Item No. 6299) e.g. cancer. Prior to July 1st, 1985, this was an unrestricted item - since then the restriction specifying medical indication has applied. Dr. Mead advises that the aim of this was to specifically address ritual female circumcision. During the years 1983, 1984 and 1985 the incidence of Item 6299 has been 11, 12 and 13 respectively. The Federal Health Department is clearly anxious to ensure that the cost of female circumcision is not underwritten through the Medicare Benefits Schedule..

Medical opinion in Australia opposes the practice of male circumcision and policy statements such as that of the Australian College of Paediatrics refer to male circumcision only. The College's policy is that it will continue to discourage the practice and "educate" parents who still opt for this choice for their male children. Female circumcision - with the possible exception of the "sunna" practice which some compare most with male circumcision, is a more drastic and serious process. This inevitably raises the question of how to approach an issue which may assume more seriousness as migration from countries which traditionally follow the custom increases.

LEGISLATION OR EDUCATION

No State or Territory in Australia has a specific Act which prohibits female genital mutilation. (This is certainly the case in Queensland, New South Wales, Western Australia, the Northern Territory, Tasmania, South Australia and the A.C.T. Victoria did not respond to enquiries. In the seven states/territories which did respond to a request for information female child circumcision is handled via existing child protection laws. Only Western Australia is formulating policies specifically concerned with female circumcision. A policy directive states that any mutilation of a child that causes short or long term effects can be considered a child protection issue. The policy states:

"Some culturally based practices such as clitorectomies contain elements that can be viewed as violating a child's rights to protection from harm. To determine whether such a practice constitutes harm, three factors must be considered:

1. Does the cultural practice violate the minimum standard of care that is the right of all children?
2. Is the practice both central to the cultural value system and normal within the culture?
3. Does the practice involve unnecessary or prolonged suffering or harm to the child?

Given these three criteria, clitorectomies can be seen to violate the child's right to protection from harm.

It is the responsibility of the Department for Community Services to investigate all specific allegations of harm to children. In this instance, the primary aim of the Department's intervention will be however to encourage informed debate about this issue, with the intention of encouraging groups or individuals to cease such practices which may lead to harm to children."

The Northern Territory Government similarly would balance any claims of religious or cultural justification against the extent and nature of maltreatment suffered.

Countries which have enacted legislation to prohibit genital mutilation - apart from those in which the practice in indigenous - are Sweden (1982), the United Kingdom (1985). Norway has legislation planned which may now be in operation.

The real question is whether legislation is effective or not or whether it simply drives the practice underground causing more pain and risk. The Prohibition of Female Circumcision Act 1985 (UK) has been criticised by children's rights groups for not going far enough and by Black Women's Health Action Project for failing to consult with the racial groups concerned. Commenting on the legislation the Children's Legal Centre wrote:

"Scope: Creates new offences for the commission of female circumcision. Section 1 makes it an offence "to excise, infibulate or otherwise mutilate the whole or any part of the labia majora or labia minora or clitoris of another person". Aiding, abetting, counselling or procuring such an act is also an offence. "Necessary surgical operations" are exempted from being an offence where such an operation "is necessary for the physical or mental health" of the person concerned. A further exemption exists where it is performed for purposes connected with childbirth.

The Act provides, however, that in determining whether an operation is necessary for the mental health of a person "no account shall be taken of the effect of that person of any belief on the part of that or any other person that the operation is required as a matter of custom or ritual."

Child Impact: The Act does not go far enough in its attempt to protect girls and women from this practice. The "mental health" criterion has been criticised both because it is discriminatory and because it could provide a loophole which diminishes the limited protection that the Act provides. It is anticipated that there may be an increase in backstreet practices."

The London based Black Women's Health Project was critical of the lack of consultation and objected to Section 2 of the Act which legalised female circumcision if deemed necessary for the physical or mental health of a woman and also made it unlawful when practised because of custom. Commenting on the Bill (before it was passed) in its latest Annual Report, they write:

"Some of the problems created by the passing of this legislation are: (a) the circumcision of mothers, who may perform the operation themselves out of compassionate concern for their daughters' future welfare and to ensure marriage within the community; (b) the growth of a backstreet industry thriving on the confusion and fears of the affected communities; (c) panic caused by a lack of understanding of the Bill and its legal implications.

We also believe that legislation will be ineffective in stopping the practice which experience has taught us can only be challenged through health education."(5)

Studying reports from women who are from and work in countries where female circumcision is common the emphasis is placed consistently on education rather than legislation. Indeed in Sudan, which forbade infibulation in 1946, the practice is still common and one study of 4,000 women in 1967 found 80% were infibulated. In 1979 another study found 80%+ of Sudanese women were infibulated. Legislation resulted in people racing to have their children infibulated to "beat" the law. It was acknowledged after this experience that education as to the effects of "that bad and cruel custom" should be education of both male and female Sudanese alike. In fact, in Sudan little has changed and pharaonic circumcision is still widely practised.

The general concensus seems to be that legislation drives the practice underground or causes earlier circumcision - as the Ethiopian experience indicates. It is suspected that since the Eritrean People's Liberation Front banned genital mutilation (1977-9) many girls from other parts of the country ran away to join the army to escape the knife!

LEGISLATION FOR AUSTRALIA?

Australia can learn from the British experience and the reactions of black women's groups opposed to circumcision with practical experience of the practice - either personally or though their work. Australia does not have the large African/Muslim population of Britain or Sweden and child female genital mutilation is not, one deduces, of the same dimension here. Neither is it easy for the average Australian to understand the immense social pressure on women to have their daughters circumcised. The Black Women's Health Action Project Group believe that it can be most effective in stopping female circumcision by stimulating debate within the cultures where it is practised and providing education about its harmful effects - a large part of this is breaking down the taboos surrounding female sexuality and circumcision.

Black women with whom the issue was discussed were confused by the British legislation and did not understand why the British Government should legislate about something which did not affect British people! A pamphlet in Somali was of great value to these women. The conclusions of the Black Women's group were:

"There is clearly still a great deal of fear concerning the abandonment of female circumcision by these women (i.e. those involved in counselling sessions). We feel that one of the principal difficulties is that women are afraid that other cultural values will suffer, so the problem is how can we abandon circumcision without affecting the status of women which is very important in Somali culture, and where the uncircumcised woman has been scorned and rejected."

CONCLUSION AND RECOMMENDATIONS

It is unlikely that Australia will see the extreme cases of female genital mutilation (i.e. infibulation) because the population of this country from countries where it is commonly practised does not compare with that of the United Kingdom. This notwithstanding it is sensible for State Welfare Departments to prepare for the few cases that may occur. There is no question that circumcision - in whatever form - of female children is maltreatment and constitutes serious physical assault. However, unlike other forms of child abuse, many parents - most often mothers - who want their daughters to be circumcised are usually motivated by concern for their daughters' marriage prospects and acceptance by the societal group particularly "back home". However, it is interesting that the most zealous supporters of female circumcision are women bound by traditional custom, some of whom, according to one Sudanese study, are motivated by spite - "we suffered, so should our children and grandchildren."

As far as South Australia is concerned - with no known cases reported - specific legislation banning the practice when the extent of it is not reported and not fully known - is premature. Existing child protection legislation, particularly Section 12(1) (Children's Protection and Young Offenders Act, 1979) provides an avenue through which protective proceedings could be taken if necessary. The World Health Organisation, UNICEF and other world bodies do not advocate legislation as a means of combating female circumcision because it is difficult to enforce and drives the practitioners underground.

It is suggested that welfare departments in the states and territories prepare policy statements for the benefit of their social workers and others (e.g. health service nurses, paediatricians) as part of their overall training policies which address the issue of female circumcision in an educative way - what is it, what does it involve. Policy should address, as does that in Western Australia, the following:

1. Does the practice involve unnecessary or prolonged suffering or harm to the child?

2. Does the practice violate a child's basic right to safety?

If the answer is 'yes' to the above, notwithstanding that the practice is seen as "normal" by the cultural group involved, then the child's right to safety and protection has been infringed. All such cases must be reported to the Department of Community Welfare but the intervention thereafter should involve women from ethnic health/community centres who can educate the families concerned about the harmful effects of female circumcision.

Sally N. McGregor
Executive Officer, Children's Interests Bureau
November, 1986.

REFERENCES

1. *"A traditional practice that threatens health - female circumcision"* World Health Organisation Chronicle 40(1):31-36 (1986).

2. *"Female Circumcision, Excision and Infibulation"* The Minority Rights Group Report No.47

3. *"Cautious Forum and Damaging Practices"* by Claire Brisset, Le Monde, 28 February and 1 March, 1979.

4. *"Medical Benefits for Circumcision - News Release from the Australian Minister of Health"* The Hon. N. Blewett.

5. London Black Women's Health Action Project, *Annual Report 1985-86.*

NOTES

1. The Minority Rights Group, Report No.47: Female Circumcision, Excision and Infibulation, p.7

2. Ibid, p.18

3. Prohibition of Female Circumcision Act 1985, Her Majesty Stationery office, p.2

4. The Hosken Report, Genital and Sexual Mutilation of Women, 1979

5. The Minority, op. cit., p.7

6. A Manual for Educators and Group Facilitators: Female Circumcision and Consciousness Raising, p.30-31

7. The Minority, op. cit., p.5

8. Olayinka Koso Thomas, The Circumcision of Women: A Strategy for Eradication, p.36

BIBLIOGRAPHY

El Dareer Asma   Woman, Why do you Weep?
Circumcision and its Consequences
Zed Press London 1982

Graham Efua and   Female Circumcision and Consciousness
Adamson Fiona   Raising.
A Manual for Group Educators and Group
Facilitators
FORWARD London

Koso-Thomas   The Circumcision of Women, A Strategy
Olayinka   for Eradication
Zed Press London 1987

Thiam Awa   Black Sisters Speak Out, Feminism and
Oppression in Black Africa.
Pluto Press London 1986

JOURNALS/NEWSPAPERS

Canadian Women
Les Cashiers
de la Femme

Campaigning Against Female
Circumcision: London Black Women's
Health Action Project, p.83-84

City Limits

British Schoolgirls Under the Knife
Simon Denison, 16-23 February 1989

Doctor

Plea to Stem Circumcision of Ethnic Girls
Paul Grinstead, The Weekly Newspaper for
the Family Practitioner, 9 February 1989,
Vol.19, No.6

Feminist Review

Under Western Eyes: Feminist Scholarship
and Colonial Discourses,
Chandra Mohanty, p.61-87, No.30,
Autumn 1988

Kick It Over

Sexual Terrorism,
Awa Thiam, Spring 1987
(Reprinted from International Social
Studies Journal, Vol.35, No.4, 1983

Monochrome

Female Circumcision is Still Prevalent in
the Arab World, in Africa and in Britain
David Smith, July 1985

Nursing Times

Racism in Nursing
Cherril Hicks, p.743-748, 5 May 1982

Observer, The

Female Mutilation: In the Name of
Tradition Alison Whyte, 5 March 1989

Scotsman, The **(Scotswoman, The)**	The Unkindest Cut of All Sue Armstrong, Thursday, 18 July 1989
Sister Links	Update: Female Circumcision Campaign, p.6 Reports: Building Bridges Across Cultures, Emily Booth, p.14-15, Vol.1, No.2, June 1985 FORWARD's Quarterly
Spur	Women Mutilated Efua Graham, p.3, May 1984
Tower Tribune	Women Condemn Circumcision Bill Sylvia Pleasant, p.3, 18 March 1985
Women's **International** **Network News** **(WIN News)**	Genital and Sexual Mutilation of Females: Groupe Femmes pour l'Abolition des Mutilations Sexuelles (GAMS) WIN News X-1 Winter 1984

DOCUMENTS/ADDITIONAL MATERIAL

Pamphlets, Leaflets, Newsletters, No.1-10; Proposal for a Film on Female Circumcision, Shamis Dirir, Joan Leese, Liliane Landau and Kia Chester, London Black Women Health Action Project.

REPORTS/PARLIAMENTARY BILLS AND ACT/ PLAN OF ACTION /POLICY/ RECOMMENDATIONS/SPEECHES

Annual Reports, London Black Women Health Action Project, 1985-1988

Report No.47, The Minority Rights Group: Female Circumcision, Excision and Infibulation, 1982

Report of the Inter-African Committee, Regional Seminar on: Traditional Practices Affecting the Health of Women and Children in Africa, Addis Abeba, 6-10 April 1987

Report on the First National Conference on Female Genital Mutilation, 1 February 1989, FORWARD

Plan of Action for the Eradication of Harmful Traditional Practices Affecting Women and Children in Africa, Inter-African Committee and Members

House of Common Official Report, Parliamentary Debates, Prohibition of Female Circumcision Bill, Wednesday, 3 April 1985, Her Majesty's Stationery Office, London 1985

Lords Debates, Prohibition of Female Circumcision Bill, 15 May 1985 and Monday, 3 June 1985

A Bill to Prohibit Female Circumcision, 1983 and 1985

Prohibition of Female Circumcision Act 1985, Chapt.38, Her Majesty's Stationery Office, London 1985

Policy Implications for Welfare Departments, Female Circumcision: A Discussion Paper, Sally N. Castell-McGregor, South Australian Children's Interest Bureau, November 1986

Recommendations on Female Circumcision Made at the Dakar Seminar, Dakar, February 1984

Speech, Mrs Aziza Kamel on the Occasion of the Meeting of the Working Group on Female Circumcision, Field Work Accomplishments Against Female Circumcision, October 1979

خاطمہ منگول

Typeset and printed by Ace Duplicating Services, London E2. 01-981 7834